Werner Held

THE
GERMAN FIGHTER
UNITS OVER RUSSIA

THE GERMAN FIGHTER UNITS OVER RUSSIA

A PICTORIAL HISTORY OF THE PILOTS AND AIRCRAFT

WERNER HELD

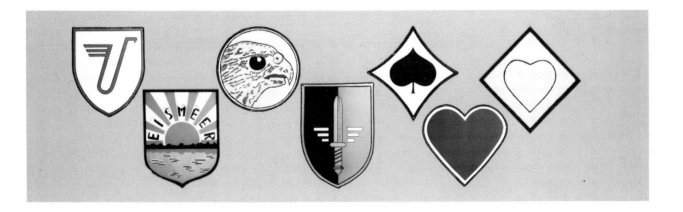

1469 Morstein Road, West Chester, Pennsylvania 19380

List of Waffen-SS Ranks and their World War II German and US Equivalents

Waffen-SS	German WWII Army	U.S. WWII Army
General Officers		
–No equivalent–	Generalfeldmarschall	General of the Army
Oberstgruppenführer	Generaloberst	General
Obergruppenführer	General	Lieutenant General
Gruppenführer	Generalleutnant	Major General
Brigadeführer	Generalmajor	Brigadier General
Staff Officers		
Oberführer	–No equivalent–	–No equivalent–
	(Wore the shoulder strap of a Colonel)	
Standartenführer	Oberst	Colonel
Obersturmführer	Oberstleutnant	Lieutenant Colonel
Sturmbannführer	Major	Major
Company Officers		
Hauptsturmführer	Hauptmann	Captain
Obersturmführer	Oberleutnant	1st Lieutenant
Untersturmführer	Leutnant	2nd Lieutenant
Officer Candidates *(Basically equal to Oberfeldwebel & Feldwebel)*		
Oberjunker	Oberfähnrich	–No equivalent–
Junker	Fähnrich	–No equivalent–
Noncommissioned Officers		
Sturmscharführer	Stabsfeldwebel	Sergeant Major
Hauptscharführer	Oberfeldwebel	Master Sergeant
Oberscharführer	Feldwebel	Technical Sergeant
Scharführer	Unterfeldwebel	Staff Sergeant
Unterscharführer	Unteroffizier	Sergeant
Enlisted Men		
–No equivalent–	Stabsgefreiter	Admin. Corporal
Rottenführer	Obergefreiter	Corporal
Sturmmann	Gefreiter	Corporal
SS-Obersoldat*	Obersoldat*	Private 1st Class
SS-Soldat*	Soldat*	Private

*Note: *Soldat* is a general term. Other words used here are Schütze, Grenadier, Füsilier, depending upon the combat arm to which the soldier belonged.

Source of U.S. World War II army equivalents: War Department Technical Manual TM-E 30-451 *Handbook on German Military Forces*, 15 March 1945.

Photographic material was provided by:

Buchner, Hermann
Dölling, Helmut
Hartmann, Erich
Hofmann, Hans
Kretschmer, Wolfgang
Losigkeit, Fritz
Nickolai, Erich
Obermaier, Ernst
Petrick, Peter
Romm, Oskar
Schnörrer, Karl
and the author's archives

Translated from the German by Dr. Edward Force,
Central Connecticut State University.

Copyright © 1990 by Schiffer Publishing.
Library of Congress Catalog Number: 90-60470.

Printed in the United States of America.
ISBN: 0-88740-246-1

This book originally published under the title,
Die Deutschen Jagdgeschwader im Russlandfeldzug,
by Podzun-Pallas Verlag, GmbH, 6360 Friedberg 3 (Dorheim) Markt 9.
© 1986. ISBN: 3-7909-0282-9.

Published by Schiffer Publishing, Ltd.
1469 Morstein Road
West Chester, Pennsylvania 19380
Please write for a free catalog.
This book may be purchased from the publisher.
Please include $2.00 postage.
Try your bookstore first.

CONTENTS

INTRODUCTION

THE FATEFUL YEARS—SACRIFICE IN THE EAST
1941-1945

When German army units crossed the eastern border between East Prussia and Rumania on June 22, 1941, they were effectively supported by three air fleets. It was the assignment of the fighter units to knock out the Soviet air forces as quickly as possible and assure aerial superiority. Surprise attacks on the enemy's airfields near the front in the morning and hard aerial fighting with swarms of I-16 and I-153 fighters in the afternoon, as well as defensive action from twin-engined Russian bomber units resulted in a successful score of 1800 enemy planes, some destroyed on the ground and some in the air, by the time fighting ended in the evening of that first day. The quickly advancing army and Panzer units always received the support they needed from the German Luftwaffe. Many experienced German fighter pilots scored ever-greater successes, and the numbers of their Knight's Cross and Oak Leaf holders grew steadily. Only after the first Russian winter began did the front come to a standstill. The front froze between Moscow and the surrounded city of Leningrad.

—

During the advance it was the pilots of Jagdgeschwader 54 *Grünherz* and the II. Group of Jagdgeschwader 53, subordinate to them until September, who had the task of securing the air space over the army units in the northern sector. Jagdgeschwader 51, along with the II. Group of JG 27 (until July 1941) and the staff and III. Group of JG 27 (until October 1941) flew in the central sector. The II. Group of JG 52 also saw service in this sector. In October the III./JG 52 joined them. In the southern sector there were Jagdgeschwader 3 and the I. and III. Groups of JG 53 and JG 77.

After the winter began, various groups moved back to Germany to rest, and some of them were later transferred to the Mediterranean. These were Jagdgeschwader 53 and 77. The II./JG 27 had already left Russia in July of 1941 and been reequipped for service in Africa. The staff and III./JG 27 followed in October.

The units that remained in Russia generally spent the rough winter months at expanded ex-Russian airfields.

The II. Group of JG 3 was transferred to the island of Sicily from January to the end of April 1942 for action against Malta, while the III. Group saw service in the northern sector of the eastern front from January to April of 1942. Only the summer offensive of 1942 united the squadron again for action in the direction of Stalingrad. Thus Jagdgeschwader 3, which was given the name of *Udet* after Ernst Udet's death, remained in eastern service. In the summer of 1943 the entire Geschwader 3 *Udet* was transferred home to defend the Reich.

In May of 1942 the Jagdgeschwader 5 *Eismeer* was formed. To the squadron staff were added the Kirkenes destroyer unit and the II. Group—the former Petsamo Jagdgruppe. The IV./JG 1 was reformed into the III./JG 5. In the summer of 1942 a newly-formed IV. Group was finally added and given the task of guarding the coast from Drontheim to Narvik. The far north of Europe—northern Norway and northern Finland—essentially remained the scene of Geschwader 5's action. The squadron's units had as their most important assignments the escorting of Stuka and bomber units that attacked Allied convoys to Murmansk. In November of 1943 the II. Group was transferred to action against Russia in the northern and central sectors, and at the end of May 1944 they were sent to protect the Reich. The I. Group was also transferred in November of 1943, at first to Rumania and finally back home to guard the Reich. The rest of the squadron remained in the Stavanger-Bergen area until the war's end.

Jagdgeschwader 51, which was called *Jagdgeschwader 51 Mölders* after the death of their former Commodore Werner Mölders, remained on duty in Russia during the first winter of the war, 1941-42. The II. Group operated since November of 1942 in the Mediterranean area, Italy, the Balkans and the Vienna area. The remaining groups were to be found at almost all the major war areas in the east during 1942, 1943 and 1944. The Jagdgeschwader Mölders was sustained by the splendid achievements of its men, who were recognized and decorated with high honors. The price in blood that their achievements cost, though, was considerable.

Jagdgeschwader 52—after a rest during the winter months—took part as a whole in the fighting in the basin south of Kharkov and finally became a purely eastern squadron during the great summer offensive of 1942. Separated from each other in space, the groups operated independently at all the major points on the front. The pilots of the squadron fought from Moscow to the Causasus, over Stalingrad and at the Kuban bridgehead until the evacuation of the Crimea in May of 1944. At the war's end, Jagdgeschwader 52 ranked first among all Jagdgeschwader in terms of their success.

Jagdgeschwader 53 *Pik As* (Ace of Spades) fought in Russia from the very beginning. While the I. Group saw action in the southern sector until the beginning of August 1941, the II. Group was subordinated to JG 54 in the northern sector and remained in that area until mid-September 1941. At the end of September the I. and II. Groups were removed from eastern service and rested on the border of The Netherlands, then were transferred to the Mediterranean. The III. Group was finally transferred there as well, and the united squadron fought over Malta and North Africa. Only the I. Group was sent back to Russia from June to September of 1942, fighting there from Kursk to Stalingrad along with the remaining eastern units.

Jagdgeschwader 54 *Grünherz* began the Russian campaign from East Prussia in the northern sector, serving from Dünaburg to shortly before Leningrad. For almost two years the three groups of this squadron operated from the formerly Russian airfields of Siverskaya, Krasnogwardeisk, Staraya-Russa and Ryelbitzi in the northern sector. At the beginning of February 1943 the III. Group was transferred to the west and defended the Reich until the war ended. In July of 1943 a IV. Group was established, which saw service along with the I. and II. Groups again and again at all the major points on the eastern front. From Finland to the

Crimea, planes with the "Green Heart" emblem could be found. Only in the spring of 1944 did the I. and II. Groups return to the northern sector. In Courland the pilots again scored great successes. At the end of the war, the remnants of the squadron were able to return from the Courland Basin to Flensburg. The IV. Group fought to defend the Reich from September of 1944 on, suffering heavy losses, and was disbanded in February of 1945.

Jagdgeschwader 77 *Herz As* (Ace of Hearts) began the campaign in Rumania. While the I. Group fought along with JG 3 in the Kiev area until the end of 1941, the other groups saw action at the extreme south of the eastern front. In the spring of 1942 the squadron was reunited and based in the Crimea. Early in July of 1942 the I. Group was transferred to the Mediterranean, while the II. Group saw action near Kursk. At the beginning of September 1942, the III. Group and the squadron staff could be found in the northern sector near Leningrad. In mid-October the groups still in Russia left the eastern front and joined the I. Group for service in the Mediterranean.

—

Tunisia, Sardinia and northern Italy were other areas of action for these groups. In 1944 the groups were in Rumania, Siebenbürgen and Vienna, until the squadron was assigned to defend the Reich and serve in the west as of October 1944. What remained of the squadron was in the Upper Silesia-Bohemia area when the war ended.

JUNE 22, 1941—
OPERATION BARBAROSSA

Pilots of Jagdgeschwader 53 in an observation tower on the eastern boundary of the Reich. One day later—on June 22, 1941—the war against Russia began.

June 22, 1941—the beginning of Operation "Barbarossa." German fighter planes over the endless plains of Russia.

Enemy airfields near the border are the targets of German bomber and dive-bomber units. The German fighters took an effective part in knocking out the Russian air force.

The Commander of the III. Group of JG 53, Hauptmann Wilcke, before taking off for action.

Oberstleutnant Werner Mölders successfully leads his Jagdgeschwader 51 against the enemy.

The *Grünherzgeschwader* JG 54, serving in the northern sector of the 1600-kilometer front, knocked 65 Soviet bombers out of the skies over Dünaburg.

The Russian I-153 and I-16 (Rata) fighters were naturally very inferior to the German Bf 109 fighters in terms of speed, but very dangerous on account of their maneuverability.

A German pilot in
an intact Rata: A
photo for the loved
ones back home.

Henschel Hs 123—
the "One-Two-
Three" was also used
in Russia in the
beginning. This craft
was the German
fighter plane in the
"first hour."

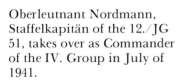

Oberleutnant Nordmann,
Staffelkapitän of the 12./JG
51, takes over as Commander
of the IV. Group in July of
1941.

Hauptmann Bretnütz—Commander of the
II./JG 53—and his group were subordinated to
JG 54 at the beginning of the eastern campaign.
He was badly wounded on June 22, 1941 after
shooting down a bomber and died in hospital
on June 27, 1941.

Squadron Adjutant JG 53—Leutnant Schiess—
takes off for action.

Three Messerschmitt
fighters of the staff of
JG 53 return from
action. The
Commodore, Major
von Maltzahn, shot
down his 40th enemy
plane in this
mission,
Oberleutnant Pufahl
his fifth and
Leutnant Schiess his
ninth.

14

The parking areas of the former Russian airfields are strewn with destroyed enemy planes.

The General of the VIII. Fliegerkorps, Baron von Richthofen, was honored with the oak leaves on July 17, 1941. The General is seen here in a Fieseler "Storch."

Hauptmann Wilhelm Spies, Commander of the I. Group of Destroyer Squadron 26, received the Knight's Cross on June 14, 1941 after ten aerial victories. In Russia too, Spies and his group were very successful.

This well-camouflaged I-153 fell into German hands.

Destroyer Squadron 1—called the Wasp Squadron—also fought on the eastern front. Although the planes generally attacked land targets, many of the pilots were able to make use of their earlier fighter training in air battles.

July 7, 1941 in Dubno—Leutnant "Bob" Preu (right) is in good spirits despite being wounded. Left: Oberleutnant Pufahl, Major von Maltzahn (center), Leutnant Schiess (second from right).

The Commodore of JG 53, Major Baron von Maltzahn (center), at the Krzewica airfield after one of his 33 eastern aerial victories.

Supplies are brought in by "Good Aunt Ju" (Ju 52). The Biala-Zerkow airfield was just behind the front at the beginning of August 1941.

Oberstleutnant Mölders (JG 51) and Generaloberst Guderian (Commander of Panzergruppe 2) discuss joint operations.

"Daddy" Mölders after landing. He was the first German fighter pilot who shot down 100 enemy planes in air battles (in the west and east).

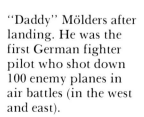

Russian tanks taken by surprise while being unloaded.

A shot-down I-16 in the northern sector of the eastern front.

An I-18 destroyed
on the ground.

The Squadron's
light plane (Fw
158) brings mail
from home. The
planes of the
II./JG 54
Grünherz are well
camouflaged.

"Hups" Mütherich, the
Staffelkapitän of the 5./JG 54,
handing out mail.

Lovingly decorated graves of fallen comrades. Here two pilots of the 4th Staffel of JG 53 rest in Russian soil.

The Commodore of JG 3, Major Lützow, at his battle station.

Major "Franzl" Lützow (center) and the Commander of the III./JG 3, Hauptmann Walter Oesau (right).

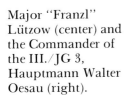

Hauptmann Oesau remained in Russia only until July of 1941. After 44 aerial victories in the east, he was called to the western defensive front as Commodore of Jagdgeschwader 2. Oesau ranks among the great unit leaders of the German Luftwaffe.

Leutnant Schiess, pilot on the staff of JG 53, after a hard aerial battle. Schiess scored 14 aerial victories in the east before he and his unit were transferred to the Mediterranean. He went missing after an aerial battle near Ischia on September 2, 1943.

Camouflaged Bf 109 planes of the 4th Staffel of JG 53 in Russia.

General der Flieger, Ritter von Greim, visits JG 53 in Turanowka. Standing at left beside the General is Commodore Major Baron von Maltzahn.

The location and battlefield of the 7th Staffel of JG 3.

Well camouflaged but always ready for action is the Bf 109 of Oberleutnant Sochatzy.

Group picture of the 7th Staffel of JG 3. Third from right: Oberleutnant Kurt Sochatzy, who was awarded the Knight's Cross on August 12, 1941 after 38 aerial victories. Nine days before, he was taken prisoner by the Russians after an IL-2 that he had shot down tore off the right wing of his plane.

This series of pictures shows
an aerial victory over an SB-2
bomber by Oberleutnant
Kurt Sochatzy.

Burial of the Knight's Cross holder and Staffelkapitän of the 6./JG 51, Oberleutnant Hans Kolbow. A last farewell from the Commodore, Oberstleutnant Mölders.

Oberleutnant Viktor Bauer, Staffelkapitän in the III. Group of JG 3, received the Knight's Cross on July 30, 1941, after 34 aerial victories.

Knight's Cross holder (since July 2, 1941) and Commander of the II. Group of JG 51, Hauptmann Josef Fözö, crashed very seriously on takeoff and was taken to a hospital back home.

Hauptmann Theodor Rossiwall, Staffelkapitän of the 5./ZG 26, is awarded the Knight's Cross by Generaloberst Keller on August 6, 1941, after ten aerial victories.

On the same day, Oberleutnant Hubert Mütherich was honored with the Knight's Cross after 31 aerial victories. Mütherich was the Staffelkapitän of the 5./JG 54 and flew in the northern sector of the eastern front.

Oberleutnant Helmut Meckel of the I./JG 3, honored on August 12 after 25 aerial victories.

Oberleutnant Horst Carganico led the renowned 6th Staffel of JG 5 on the Arctic front. In April of 1952 he became the Commander of the II. Group of this squadron. In May of 1944 Carganico crashed fatally while landing. He had brought down a total of 60 enemy planes.

Oberleutnant Max Buchholz, also of the I./JG 3, received the Knight's Cross on August 12, 1941, after 27 aerial victories.

Leutnant Hugo Dahmer (6./JG 5) received the Knight's Cross after 22 aerial victories.

Staffelkapitän Oberleutnant Horst Carganico warms the seat of his pants on his Bf 109. His crew rejoices with their captain, who was honored with the Knight's Cross on September 25, 1941 after 27 victorious air battles.

Hauptmann Kurt Ubben led the III. Group of JG 77 in Russia since the end of September 1941. He received the Knight's Cross as Staffelkapitän of the 8./JG 77 on September 4, 1941, after 28 aerial victories. Kurt Ubben died in the west on April 27, 1944 as Commodore of Jagdgeschwader 2 *Richthofen*. In all, he scored 110 aerial victories, some 90 of them in the east.

Oberleutnant Karl-Heinz Leesmann was a Group Commander in JG 52 when he received the Knight's Cross on July 23, 1941 after 22 aerial victories. Leesmann fell on July 27, 1943 as Commander of the III./JG 1, while defending the Reich. He scored 37 aerial victories, 15 of them in the west.

Hauptmann Rolf Kaldrack led the II./SKG (Schnellkampf-geschwader) 210 in Russia and was able to defeat ten enemies. He fell on February 3, 1942 after a total of 21 aerial victories. The oak leaves were conferred on Hauptmann Kaldrack posthumously.

Hauptmann Joppien already wore the oak leaves when he came to Russia with Werner Mölders as Group Commander of the I./JG 51. On August 25, 1941 he crashed fatally during an aerial battle near Brjansk. He shot down 28 enemy planes in the east.

The "White 4" of the 8th Staffel, JG 3.

Leutnant Schiess at the Biala-Zerkow front airfield on August 6, 1941. On 87 missions he was able to bring down nine bombers and five fighters of the enemy.

Leutnant Steindl, Adjutant of the II./JG 54, in flight on a fighter-bomber mission. The 250-kilogram bomb slung under the plane is readily visible.

On September 9, 1941 Oberleutnant Mütherich died in a crash-landing. For a short time, Leutnant Ostermann took command of the 5th Staffel. Left: Mütherich; right: Oberleutnant Wolfgang Späte, who subsequently led the Staffel. Späte received the Knight's Cross on October 5 after 45 aerial victories.

Oberleutnant Franz Beyer
led the 8th Staffel of JG 3
since July of 1941. On
August 30, 1941 he received
the Knight's Cross after 32
aerial victories. In June of
1943 he organized the IV.
Sturm/JG 3 for the defense
of the Reich, and he fell at
Venlo, Holland on
February 11, 1944. He
scored about 70 of his 81
aerial victories in Russia.

A "weapon mixer" of the
8./JG 3 servicing the guns.

Hauptmann Wolf-Dietrich Wilcke, Commander of the III./JG 53, came to the eastern front after scoring 13 victories in the west, and received the Knight's Cross on August 6, 1941, after 25 aerial victories. From December 1941 to May 1942 his group fought in the Mediterranean area. Then Wilcke returned to the staff of JG 3 in Russia. In December of 1942 he became Commodore of JG 3. On December 23, 1942, as a Major, he received the crossed swords after 155 aerial victories.

Hauptmann Franz von Werra—a name that became renowned for his adventurous flight from captivity in Canada. Since the summer of 1941 von Werra served as Commander of the I./JG 53 in Russia, where he was able to shoot down 13 Russian planes before his fatal accident at Vlissingen on October 25, 1941. Franz von Werra, wearing the Knight's Cross, stands at the center of this picture.

Oberfeldwebel Stefan Litjens, pilot of the 4th Staffel of JG 53, was shot down by anti-aircraft fire on the Leningrad front on September 11, 1941 and lost his right eye. Nevertheless, he flew again in the Mediterranean area and in defense of the Reich as of November 1942. After shooting down two four-engined planes, he injured his left eye in a crash landing and had to give up active duty. Litjens was honored with the Knight's Cross while in a hospital on June 21, 1943.

Werner Mölders—promoted to First General of the Jagdflieger after his 101st aerial victory—talking with Generalfeldmarschall Kesselring.

General of the Jagdflieger, Oberst Werner Mölders, with the III./JG 3; at left is Oberleutnant "Pitt" Mertens.

Officers of JG 54 *Grünherz* and the II./JG 53, which was subordinate to it, in the northern sector. At left is Commodore Trautloft.

Major Hannes Trautloft, Commodore of the *Grünherz* fighters, on the Leningrad front. Trautloft, an experienced fighter pilot and group leader, received the Knight's Cross on July 27, 1941 after 20 aerial victories. Among his total of 27 victories were four from the Spanish Civil War (Condor Legion).

The JG 54 *Grünherz* occupied the former Russian airfields of Siverskaya, Krasnogwardeisk (Gatschina), Staraja-Russa and Ryelbitzi. These fields were used as bases of action by the squadron for almost two years. The pictures show the field at Krasnogwardeisk.

An aerial photo of the Summer Palace in Gatschina, built and lived in by the Russian Tsars. Not only did the pilots of JG 54 live here, but so, at times, did personnel of various Stuka and Kampfflieger units.

Fragmentation boxes on the ring road at Krasnogwardeisk.

A Bf 109 landing at Krasnogwardeisk after a fighter-bomber mission. The pictures very clearly show the bomb carriers between the plane's landing gear.

Leutnant Max-Helmuth Ostermann (center), one of JG 54's great experts. Ostermann led the 7th Staffel until his death on August 9, 1942. In all, Ostermann shored 102 aerial victories, 93 of them in the east. He received the crossed swords on May 17, 1942, after 100 victories.

In the winter months of 1941-42, a Stuka
unit of St.G. 2 *Immelmann* also took up
quarters in Siverskaya. Their missions
covered the Grünherz planes from
Russian surprise attacks.

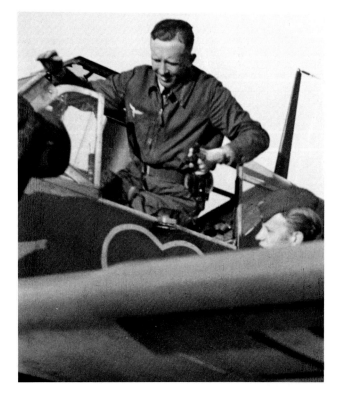

As a Schwarmführer in the 1st Staffel of
JG 54, Feldwebel Ademeit did a
particularly fine job. With prudence he
led the newly-trained pilots entrusted to
him into the air war. In 1943 and 1944
Ademeit joined the ranks of the most
successful *Grünherz* pilots.

Hauptmann Arnold Lignitz led the III./JG 54 as its Commander since October of 1940. He was one of the first members of the squadron to wear the Knight's Cross, and came to Russia after shooting down 22 planes in the west. On September 30, 1941 he had to parachute from his plane in an aerial battle with Russian fighters, and has been missing ever since.

Oberst Werner Mölders, first General of the Jagdflieger, crashed fatally in an He 111 en route to Germany on November 22, 1941. His death was a painful loss, not only for his comrades. His former squadron JG 51 was subsequently given the traditional name *Jagdgeschwader Mölders*. At left in the photo is Hauptmann Nordmann, Commander of IV./JG 51; center: Oberst Mölders; at right: Major Lützow, Commodore of JG 3.

Hauptmann Wolfgang Schenk originally led Erprobungsstaffel 210 in Russia, and became Commander of the I./ZG 1 on January 1, 1942. As a destroyer pilot, he won a total of 18 aerial victories. As a Hauptmann, Schenk received the oak leaves on October 30, 1942. As the end of the war he was the Inspector of Jet Planes. In this picture Schenk is the pilot of an Me 109.

A discussion at Siverskaya between Commodore Trautloft (JG 54) and Hauptmann Spies (Commander I./ZG 26). In the background, from top to bottom, are the emblems of the Staff Company, the II. and III. of JG 54.

Bombs for Ju 88 bombers (in the background). In the left foreground is an Hs 126 short-range reconnaissance plane.

Leutnant Georg Seelmann—Staffelkapitän of the II./JG 51—received the Knight's Cross on October 6, 1941 after 37 aerial victories. As of May 1943, Seelmann was transferred to training groups as an instructor.

Oberleutnant Erich Hohagen received the Knight's Cross on October 5, 1941, after scoring 30 aerial victories with the 4./JG 51. In the three months that he served in Russia, Hohagen shot down 20 enemy planes.

General Paulus (center) at a combat briefing with officers of the *Jagdgeschwader Mölders*. At the far right is Oberleutnant Heinz Bär.

An undamaged Ilyushin IL-4 fell into German hands at Bobruisk. During the entire World War II era this plane was the standard medium-heavy bomber of the Red Air Force. Because of its great range, the IL-4 was the first Russian plane to fly missions against Berlin. In the last months of the war, the plane was used as a torpedo bomber over the Baltic Sea.

The *Eismeer-Geschwader* JG 5 was given a destroyer unit, which was designated 10.(Z)JG 5. This unit flew special escort missions over great distances. Special bombing missions of He 111 Heinkel bombers against the Russian supply harbor in Murmansk were possible only with an Me 110 as an escort. The planes of this Staffel carried the symbol of a dachshund eating airplanes.

Oberleutnant Brandis (right) and Radioman Baus with the score of their aerial victories painted on a fin. In the winter of 1941-42 they shot down 14 planes. The brave team fell on February 2, 1942.

A captured Russian I-153 fighter. This small, maneuverable plane was also used as a fighter-bomber and was still in service in 1942. The two sets of four bombs hung under it can be seen in the picture.

Here is the I-16 "Rata", badly damaged in this case, but a plane that could be very dangerous in combat because if its great maneuverability. This small plane could carry two sets of three rockets.

In intact captured Rata I-16 was painted with the German emblem.

Major Günther Lützow, Commodore of JG 3, was one of the great leaders of the German fliers. He received the oak leaves in Russia on July 20, 1941 after 42 aerial victories, and as early as October 11, 1941 his 92 victories won him the crossed swords.

The interesting painting of Lützow's Me 109 after he received the Knight's Cross at the English Channel on September 18, 1940.

Lützow's 100th aerial victory—his 77th in Russia—was won on October 24, 1941. The rudder was painted with the impressive score for the sake of the press and war correspondents.

Feldwebel Horst
Ademeit ready for
fighter-bomber
combat.

The I. Group of JG 54 built themselves a
sauna that they were happy to use. In
addition to the sauna, the Siverskaya
airfield also had a movie theater.

Unteroffizier Dürkop shows his comrade
Hein Bruhn how good he still feels after
landing.

The front that came to a standstill before the defenses around Leningrad did not remain quiet. Enemy attacks at various places made Luftwaffe action necessary in even the coldest weather. Swarms of *Grünherz* fighters carried bombs to the scenes of action. These pictures show the "black gang" hard at work.

Oberleutnant Wolfgang Späte, Staffelkapitän of the 5./JG 54, with his unit at Staraya-Russa. Späte had received the Knight's Cross on October 5, 1941, after 45 aerial victories.

As light snow falls, a Bf 109 prepares to take off. This was no flying weather for the reconnaissance men with their Hs 126 planes.

2-cm anti-aircraft guns are at the edge of the airfield, ready to take immediate action against the Soviets in case of surprise attacks.

Weapon and motor servicing by the I./JG 51 crew. The bitter cold was no reason to sit down on a hot stove. At first the "mill" at least had to be ready for service.

In the northern sector, the men—here those of the II./JG 54—were often shown where they were by road signs. Petersburg (Leningrad) was not far away.

Major Friedrich Beckh was chosen to lead the Jagdgeschwader 51 *Mölders* after the death of Werner Mölders. He led it until April 10, 1942, then served for a

Snowstorms brought all air activity to a standstill.

short time at the Reich Air Ministry in Berlin. On June 3, 1942 he became Commodore of JG 52, and went missing after a mission east of Kharkov ended in a crash-landing. (He won the Knight's Cross on September 18, 1941, after 27 aerial victories.) At left in the picture is the Commander of the III./ JG 51, Hauptmann Richard Leppla.

Fighter-bombers of
JG 51 are prepared
for combat.

Hauptmann
Leppla and
Hauptmann
Karlfried
Nordmann,
Commander of the
IV./JG 51, eating
lunch. After Beckh,
Nordmann took
command of JG 51
Mölders.

The newly appointed Inspector of Jagdflieger (Gd.J),
Adolf Galland, visited the eastern squadrons in the
winter of 1941-42. Along with Major Werner Andres,
who belonged to Galland's staff, the General learns of
the problems and needs of the units. These pictures
were taken on his visit to JG 51 *Mölders* at
Wyasma-South.

A Russian IL 2 "Butcher" taking off at Siverskaya. The alarm group took off and shot down an enemy plane over the field.

Major Dietrich Hrabak (right) led the II. Group of the *Grünherz* Geschwader until the end of October 1942, then took over as Commodore of the renowned JG 52.

The first aerial victory of the later Knight's Cross holder Karl (Quax) Schnörrer on December 31, 1941. Schnörrer later flew in the famous Novotny unit. This picture of the smiling "Quax" was taken while he served with the Ergänzungsstaffel of JG 54

A defective Me 109 is pushed
into the hangar by man
strength.

Hauptmann Hans Philipp was
the first member of JG 54 to
wear the oak leaves. After 62
aerial victories, the Kapitän of
the 4th Staffel won this
decoration. "Fips" had already
seen service with his squadron
in Poland, where he shot down
his first enemy.

The plane of a successful (30 aerial victories) pilot needs loving care from the mechanics—this one is going to the repair shop.

On January 27, 1942 the Commander of the I./ZG 26, Major Wilhelm Spies, fell during a low-level attack near Suchinitshi. After a total of 20 victories, ten in the east, this brave soldier lost his life. The picture shows Spies—still a Hauptmann— after 19 victories. The oak leaves were awarded to Major Spies Posthumously.

JG 54 also suffered a bitter loss. Hauptmann Franz Eckerle, Commander of the I./JG 54, had to crash-land beyond the front near Welikiye-Luki on February 14, 1942 after being hit, and has been missing since then. A well-known acrobatic flier before the war, Eckerle was very popular in his squadron because of his humanity and bravery. Hauptmann Eckerle also received the oak leaves, after 59 aerial victories.

During the Volkov battle—January 13 to July 27, 1942—pilots of JG 54 flew night missions against Russian supply flights. Without suffering any losses, they scored 56 aerial victories. Leutnant Leykauf (left) was one of the most successful "night hunters", with eight victories.

Air transport units supplied the units of the II. Army Corps enclosed in the basins of Colm and Demyansk (Colm as of January 21, 1942, Demyansk from February 9 to October 31, 1942).

Aerial protection for the heavily laden Ju's was provided by the fighters of JG 54 *Grünherz* and JG 51 *Mölders*. The severe cold demanded the greatest effort and sacrifice from the pilots and ground crews.

These pictures clearly show the tremendous effort as well as the great sacrifice made
from outside to provide the surrounded army units with men, ammunition and supplies.

A last briefing between Hauptmann Wilhelm Hachfeld (Commander I./JG 51) and Leutnant Erwin Fleig (at right).

A typical winter picture at an airfield in the war zone.

The JG 3 Adjutant's Me 109.

The destroyer pilots also had a hard time in the severe winter. The enemy constantly tried to penetrate the German army positions. The Bf 109 destroyers attacked with their bombs and guns.

A crew of the I. Group of ZG 1 had to crash-land. A terrible fate, especially when it had to be done behind the Russian lines.

Bf 110 planes of the II./ZG 26 in action.

Two Messerschmitt fighters of JG 51 about to take off at Terespol. In the background, a Ju 188 rolls down the runway.

An Me 321 that landed at Chatalovke attracted much attention. It had been tested in March of 1941 but was not often used as a freight glider. The main problem was the lack of a suitable towplane. At that time only the Ju 90 was capable of getting the big glider into the air. Only the development of the He 111 Z—two He 111's built as one—gave good results.

DEEP IN RUSSIA—
SUMMER 1942

Hauptmann Hans Philipp took command of the I. Group in February of 1942, on the death of its previous Commander, Hauptmann Eckerle. The Commander of the II. Group, Hrabak, wishes Hauptmann Philipp luck in his new assignment.

Leutnant Wolfgang von Kalckreuth, pilot in the 10./JG 51, was shot down in an aerial battle east of Duchovschtschina; his plane smashed deep into the ground.

Staffelkapitän of the 5./JG 51, Leutnant Hans Strelow, had to crash-land beyond the front near Mzensk on May 22, 1942 and committed suicide in the cockpit of his Me 109. On March 24, 1942 this brave soldier was decorated with the oak leaves after 66 aerial victories. In all, he won 68 victories in the east.

Hauptmann Johannes Steinhoff, until then Kapitän of the 4./JG 52, took over the leadership of the II. Group in February of 1942. As an Oberleutnant, he was awarded the Knight's Cross on August 31, 1942, having scored 100 aerial victories.

Feldwebel Leopold Steinbatz, pilot and Rottenflieger in the 9th Staffel of JG 52 with Hermann Graf, received the Knight's Cross on February 14, 1942 (42 victories) and the oak leaves on June 2, 1942 (83 victories). Steinbatz, who fell on June 15, 1942, was honored posthumously with the crossed swords on June 23, 1942, at the rank of Leutnant, having scored 99 victories.

Leutnant Gerhard Köppen of the
7./JG 52 won his 72nd aerial victory
on February 27, 1942 and was
honored with the oak leaves.

Major Hubertus von Bonin led the
III./JG 52 in the east from July 1,
1941 to June of 1943. He scored his
first four aerial victories in Spain
with the *Legion Condor*, and gained
the Knight's Cross on December 21,
1942, after 51 aerial victories.

Four successful fighter pilots of the JG 51 *Mölders*. From left to right, Hauptmann Krafft, Hauptmann Bär, Leutnant Fleig and Oberfeldwebel Höfemeier.

The camouflaged plane of the Commodore (Major Nordmann) at Schatalovka.

As everywhere in Russia, the "black gang" of JG 5 did their duty in the far north and kept the planes ready for action.

Feldwebel Rudolf Müller, pilot in the 6th Staffel of JG 5, about to begin a mission on the polar front.

Flying over the endless snow-covered landscape of the Arctic Ocean.

Hauptmann Günther Scholz led the III./JG 5 from January 1942 to June 1943, then served as Commodore of JG 5 until May of 1944. Afterward he took over the leadership of the squadron again in February of 1945, a position he held till the war's end. Scholz was probably the German fighter officer who spent the longest time of service in the same squadron.

Group Commander Hauptmann Scholz in action.

Escort service for Ju 87 Stukas
in the far north.

Hauptmann Hans Philipp,
Commander of I./JG 54,
brought down his 100th
opponent on March 31, 1942.
He was awarded the crossed
swords on March 12, 1942 after
82 aerial victories.

Hauptmann Hachfeld (left) left JG 51 in May of 1942. His successor was Hauptmann Krafft, who received the Knight's Cross (for 46 aerial victories) on March 18, 1942. Hachfeld took command of the III./ZG 2 in North Africa. He received the Knight's Cross on October 29, 1942 and crashed fatally in Bizerte on December 2, 1942.

Leutnant Hans Beisswenger was awarded the Knight's Cross by General Förster on May 9, 1942, after 47 aerial victories, and received the oak leaves after his 100th triumph. As Staffelkapitän of the 6./JG 54, Beisswenger went missing in the Ilmensee area on March 6, 1943, after scoring 152 aerial victories.

Leutnant Gerhard Köppen did not return from an aerial battle over the Sea of Azov on May 5, 1942. He had scored 85 aerial victories.

Leutnant Horst Hannig received the Knight's Cross along with Beisswenger on May 9, 1942, having scored 48 victories. This picture shows Lt. Hannig (right) with Oberleutnant Wandel in Ryelbitzi.

On May 29, 1942 Leutnant Erwin Fleig, Kapitän of the II./JG 51, had to parachute out of his plane after being hit, and was taken prisoner by the Russians. Fleig scored 66 aerial victories in all.

The destroyer units that saw service in Russia are rightfully known as the "firemen" of ground warfare. Before German attacks on Russian positions, or when Russian units had overrun the German trenches, the Me 110 or Ju 88 destroyers attacked with guns and bombs.

Leutnant Herbert Kutscha of the II. Group of Schnellkampfgeschwader 210, serving in Russia, received the Knight's Cross on September 24, 1942 after 21 aerial victories.

Oberleutnant Johannes Kiel was especially successful as a pilot in the I./ZG 26. He received the Knight's Cross on march 18, 1942 after 20 aerial victories. He was also able to destroy 62 enemy planes on the ground. Kiel crashed fatally at the end of January 1944 as Commander of the III./ZG 76 while defending the Reich.

Leutnant Heinrich Ehrler scored his 32nd aerial victory in July of 1942. At the time Ehrler flew in the 6th Staffel of JG 5 at Petsamo, Finland. As of August 1942 he led the 6th Staffel, and on October 21, 1942 he received the Knight's Cross after 41 aerial victories.

A Bf 109 of the 6th Staffel of JG 5, taking off and in the air near Petsamo.

Oberfeldwebel Otto Wessling received the Knight's Cross on September 3, 1942, after 50 aerial victories. In the Summer of 1942 he flew in the 9th Staffel of JG 3 *Udet*. In the autumn of 1943 he became Staffelkapitän of the 11./JG 3, defending the Reich, and he fell near Eschwege on April 19, 1944. He scored 83 aerial victories in all, some 70 of them in Russia. Wessling was awarded the oak leaves posthumously.

Oberfeldwebel Georg Schentke (left), also of the 9./JG 3, received the Knight's Cross on September 4, 1941. On December 25, 1942 he flew with the Platzschutzstaffel Pitomnik at Stalingrad and had to parachute out over the basin. He has been listed as missing since then. He scored at least 87 aerial victories. At right is Oberfeldwebel Eberhard von Boremsky (Knight's Cross May 3, 1942, after 43 aerial victories).

Hauptmann Wolfgang Ewald (center) served as Commander of the III./JG 3 since May of 1942. On December 9, 1942, at the rank of Major, he received the Knight's Cross after 50 aerial victories.

In Stalingrad the German 6th Army was meanwhile surrounded. Bitter fighting raged in the city. The Pitomnik supply airfield in the Stalingrad Basin could be held only until January 16, 1943; its loss sealed the fate of the army once and for all.

The railway loop in Stalingrad, called "the tennis racket" by the German pilots, served as a navigational landmark.

Pilot Hermann Graf—a name that became known in military reports in a very short time. Here are the dates of his successes in brief: Knight's Cross as Leutnant after 42 aerial victories, January 24, 1942. Oak leaves after 104 aerial victories on May 17, 1942.
Crossed swords after 106 aerial victories on May 19, 1942.
Jewels after 172 aerial victories on September 16, 1942.
200th aerial victories on October 2, 1942, at the rank of Major.

The tailfin of Hermann Graf's plane at Rogane on May 17, 1942, after his 104th victory.

On May 19, 1942 Graf shot down a Pe-3 bomber and received the crossed swords. The Commander of the III./JG 52, Hauptmann von Bonin (left), congratulates him.

On the Arctic front Feldwebel
Rudi Müller of the 6th Staffel of
JG 5 received the Knight's Cross
after 41 aerial victories; General
Stumpff (center) congratulates
him.

A swarm of JG 51 *Mölders* planes on a "free mission."

The staff swarm of JG 3 *Udet*.

Oberleutnant Viktor Bauer, III./JG 3, defeated his 100th opponent on July 25, 1942 and received the oak leaves on July 26.

In 1942 an Italian fighter unit was briefly in service on the eastern front. The Italians flew their Macchi C 200 to provide an escort for Stukas and bomber units.

Hauptmann Kurt Ubben, Commander of the III./JG 77. He received the oak leaves on March 12, 1942 after 69 aerial victories, and fell on April 27, 1944 in France, as Commodore of JG 2, after 100 victories.

Oberleutnant Heinrich Setz was Staffelkapitän of the 4./JG 77 when he received the oak leaves on June 23, 1942, after 76 aerial victories. Setz fell in the defense of the Reich on March 13, 1943, as Commander of the I./JG 27, after scoring 138 aerial victories.

Oberleutnant Erwin Clausen, Kapitän of the 6./JG 77 as of July 1942, scored his 101st aerial victory on July 23, 1942 and received the oak leaves. Clausen fell on October 4, 1943 in the defense of the Reich, as Commander of the I./JG 11, with a total of 132 victories.

Oberleutnant Siegfried Freytag received the Knight's Cross on July 3, 1942, after 49 aerial victories. At this time he flew in the I./JG 77. In all, Freytag scored 102 aerial victories, some 70 of them in Russia. As Commander of the II./JG 77 he shot down 17 English planes in one month over Malta. He ended the war in JG 7.

Weapons loaders of the III./JG 54 *Grünherz* at work.

Bf 109 0f the 8th Staffel of JG 54 before takeoff.

The "Red 1" of Leutnant Walter Nowotny, 3./JG 54, was hit hard in an aerial battle. While landing, the wings of the plane were hit by anti-aircraft fire, and the plane turned over. Nowotny remained uninjured.

The appearance of Russian aircraft changed considerably. This MiG-3 fighter fell into German hands unharmed when the pilot became disoriented and landed on a German airfield.

A shot-down IL-2 before the hangars at Ryelbitzi.

On August 2, 1942 Leutnant Nowotny scored seven aerial victories and, after 56 victories, received the Knight's Cross on September 4, 1942.

Squadron Commodore of JG 77, Major Gordon Gollob, fought with his unit in the southern sector of the eastern front. On June 24, 1942, after 107 aerial victories, Gollob received the crossed swords.

On August 14, 1942 his plane's rudder showed his score of 120 victories, and by August 30 the score was 150. Now Major Gollob was decorated with the jewels.

The Major, born in Vienna, had not only courage but humor as well. Here he relaxes and talks with his comrades.

Stukas have gathered over the scene of action, accompanied to the front by fighter planes.

The Ju 87's fly wing-tip to wing-tip. The bombs can be seen clearly under the fuselage and wings.

When Russian fighters tried to attack the unit, the Me 109's were on the scene at once, and one of the attackers is already burning.

Major Hannes Trautloft (left) speaks to the pilots of the I./JG 51. On many occasions, entire groups of one squadron were briefly subordinated to another squadron. Behind Major Trautloft stands Hauptmann Ganz, at right in Hauptmann Hachfeld, Commander of the I./JG 51. Shortly thereafter, Hachfeld went to North Africa as Commander of the III./ZG 2, where he lost his life on December 2, 1942.

Oberleutnant Hans Beisswenger
shortly before being awarded the oak
leaves on September 30, 1942, after
100 aerial victories.

Oberleutnant Adolf Dickfeld flew in the I.
Group of JG 52 and received the oak leaves on
May 19, 1942, after 101 aerial victories. Dickfeld
scored a total of 136 victories, 115 of them on
the eastern front alone.

Hauptmann Rudolf Resch received the Knight's
Cross on September 6, 1942, after 50 aerial
victories. Resch fell at Orel on July 11, 1943
after 93 victories. At that time he was the
Commander of the IV./JG 51.

Feldwebel Fredrich Wachowiak received the Knight's Cross as an Unteroffizier of the III./JG 52 in Russia on April 5, 1942. He scored at least 86 aerial victories in the east before he was transferred to the III./JG 3 in the west. He fell on the invasion front on July 16, 1944, with the rank of Leutnant.

Photographed in front of a "Storch" are, left to right, Leutnant Bürk, Oberfeldwebel Wachowiak and Major Schmitz.

Thirsty days in the late summer of 1942—a splendid "snapshot"—or "Schnapps-shot?"

Although the Knights' Cross was not awarded according to any set plan, the units generally took the right course. On such occasions, as here in JG 51, a vehicle was decorated to receive the pilot.

Two Oberfeldwebel of the II./JG 51 *Mölders* received the Knight's Cross on March 19, 1942. Left: Oberfeldwebel Otto Tange (41 victories), and right: Wilhelm Mink (40 victories). Tange fell on July 30, 1943, sustaining a direct anti-aircraft hit in Russian and Mink on March 12, 1945 in Denmark.

In August of 1942 Oberstleutnant Lützow turned the command of the JG 3 *Udet* over to Major Wolf-Dietrich Wilcke. Günther Lützow became an Inspector on the staff of the General of the Jagdflieger.

As an Unteroffizier, Karl Gratz received the Knight's Cross after 54 aerial victories. Until February of 1943 he flew in the 8th Staffel of JG 52 in Russia, and was then transferred for barely a year to the 11./JG 2 in the west, where he scored another 17 victories. Returning to his old III./JG 52, he scored a total of 138 aerial victories by the end of the war.

Hans Dammers of the 9./JG 52 was rammed by a crashing opponent on March 13, 1944 and died of the severe injuries he sustained. He had received the Knight's Cross on August 23, 1942 after 51 aerial victories as an Unteroffizier. In all, he triumphed over 113 enemies in aerial battles.

Hauptmann Joachim Wandel, Staffelkapitän of the 5./JG 54, was decorated with the Knight's Cross on August 21, 1942, after 64 aerial victories. He fell on October 7, 1942 southeast of the Ilmensee, after his 75th victory.

Oberfeldwebel Karl Hammerl of the 1st Staffel of JG 52 scored his 50th aerial victory in Russia on September 19, 1942. He went missing after a crash-landing behind the Russian lines on March 2, 1943.

Hauptmann Kurt Brändle achieved his 100th aerial victory on August 27, 1942 and was honored with the oak leaves. As of May 1942 he was the Commander of the II. Group of JG 3 *Udet*. Hauptmann Brändle fell in the west on November 3, 1943 while defending against American bombers near Amsterdam. He scored a total of 180 aerial victories, 20 of them in the west.

Kurt Brändle, meanwhile promoted to Major, after the 500th victory of his II. Group of JG 3.

Changing the engine of an Me 109 in the Ukraine. At right is Major Brändle.

Oberleutnant Helmut Mertens, I./JG 3, scored his 50th aerial victory on September 4, 1942 and was honored with the Knight's Cross. "Pitt" Mertens scored a total of 97 aerial victories and survived the war's end as Commander of the III./Ergänzungs-Jagdgeschwader 1.

Feldwebel "Toni" Hafner after being
awarded the Knight's Cross—this oversize
example made by his comrades—on
September 23, 1942 in Orel (60 aerial
victories). Hafner received the oak leaves as
a Leutnant on April 11, 1944, after 134
victories. He fell on October 17, 1944 in
East Prussia, after a total of 204 victories.
Hafner was the most successful fighter
pilot of JG 51 *Mölders*.

Major Hannes Trautloft after his 500th
mission. Trautloft was called to the staff of
the General of the Jagdflieger as
"Inspizient Ost" on July 5, 1943, after
serving as Commodore of JG 54 for almost
three years. Of his total of 57 aerial
victories, 45 were scored in Russia.

Pistol marksmanship in Krasnogwardeisk.
From left to right: Döbele, Dürkop,
Oberleutnant Lange, Raupach, Bruhn,
Ademeit. Oberleutnant Lange, who was
transferred to the 3./JG 51 as
Staffelkapitän on October 25, 1943, turned
command of his 1st Staffel of JG 54 over to
Leutnant Nowotny.

Hauptmann Günther Rall, Staffelkapitän of the 8./JG 52—scored his 100th aerial victory on October 26, 1942 and was honored with the oak leaves. In April of 1943 he took command of the III./JG 52.

The emblems of the 8./JG 5.

Feldwebel Heinrich Bartels, as a member of the 8th Staffel of JG 5, scored 45 aerial victories on the Arctic front and was honored with the Knight's Cross on November 13, 1942. In the summer of 1943 he was transferred to JG 27 and fell at Bonn on December 23, 1944, after shooting down his 99th opponent.

A swarm of the 8./JG 5 returns to Petsamo.

When Theodor Weissenberger was transferred from Zerstörerstaffel JG 77 to the II./JG 5, he had scored 23 aerial victories as a destroyer pilot. On November 23, 1942, as a Leutnant, he received the Knight's Cross after 38 victories. In June of 1943 he became Staffelkapitän of the 7./JG 5.

Oberleutnant Joachim Kirschner received the Knight's Cross as a Leutnant on December 23, 1942 after 51 aerial victories, and the oak leaves as an Oberleutnant on August 2, 1943 (170 victories). Kirschner was shot by Croatian partisans after parachuting on December 12, 1943, as Hauptmann and Commander of the IV./JG 27. He scored a total of 188 victories.

Oberleutnant Werner Lucas also gained the Knight's Cross as a member of JG 3 (September 19, 1942, after 52 victories). He was shot down over Holland on October 24, 1943. He scored 106 victories in all, about 100 of them in Russia.

Leutnant Leopold Münster, II./JG 3 *Udet*, received the Knight's Cross on December 21, 1942, after 52 aerial victories. Münster lost his life on May 8, 1944 in the defense of the Reich, while ramming a four-engine bomber. He scored 95 victories in all, some 25 in the west, and was awarded the oak leaves posthumously on May 12, 1944.

Oberleutnant Hans Götz, Staffelkapitän of the 2./JG 54, was decorated with the Knight's Cross on December 23m 1942, after 48 aerial victories. Götz fell near Karatschev, Russia on August 4, 1943, after scoring 82 victories.

In the winter of 1942-43 the first big Me 323 "Gigant" planes landed at the Witebsk airfield. These big birds were powered by six Gnome-Rhone motors (each of 1180 HP) and could carry up to 130 soldiers or 9760 kg of freight. The plane had a wingspan of 55 meters and measured 28.5 meters in length.

The I. Group of JG 51 *Mölders* was first supplied with the new Focke-Wulf Fw 190 A-3 at Jesau, East Prussia in September of 1942. In February of 1943 the pilots of the I. Group of JG 54 "Grünherz" were given the Fw 190 A-3 at Heiligenbeil. Pilots and ground crews soon familiarized themselves with the new planes. The powerful BMW 801 double-row radial engines and the wide, strong landing gear were superior to the Bf 109 on the often makeshift fields in the east. In addition, the view from the cockpit was better, as was the air-cooled motor. Both pictures of the Fw 190 A-3—planes of the I. Group of JG 54—clearly show these strong points.

Hauptmann Heinrich Krafft, Commander of the I./JG51, was shot down by Russian anti-aircraft fire near Belyj on December 14, 1942. He had scored 78 aerial victories.

Two swarms of JG 51 planes return in formation to the snow-covered airfield.

Oberleutnant Max Stotz scored ten aerial victories at Ilmensee on December 30, 1942 and defeated his 150th opponent on January 26, 1943. Stotz received the oak leaves on October 30, 1942, after 100 victories. The brave Austrian fighter pilot went missing after parachuting over Russia on August 19, 1943.

A typical winter scene on the Krasnogwardeisk airfield. Russian volunteers bring loads of fuel to the airfield on horse-drawn sleds.

Leutnant Nowotny (left), Staffelkapitän of the 1st Staffel of JG 54, with his Katschmarek
Feldwebel "Toni" Döbele. Along with Döbele, Rudi Rademacher and "Quax"
Schnörrer also flew in Nowotny's renowned swarm.

THE EASTERN WAR—
FROM THE PHOTO DIARY OF AN AMATEUR PHOTOGRAPHER
ON HIS UNIT IN THE II. GROUP OF JG 52

The red devil of the "Rabatz-Staffel", Staffel 5 of the II. Group of JG 52.

These unique pictures, taken by one of the "black gang" of the 5th Staffel of Jagdgeschwader 52 with his own camera, deserve to be presented as a unit because of their great expressiveness. The good quality of the photos— naturally, only a small selection can be shown here—document all that the photographer regarded as important in this campaign. They show in particular the unity of the ground crews with the pilots, and make very clear the admiration of the "little men" for the pilots' achievements. These pictures scarcely need a text, for they speak for themselves.

A crowded war-zone airfield at Lepel (July 7-13, 1941).

Captured and
damaged enemy
planes.

A Bf 109 of the 5th Staffel of JG 52 comes in to land.

The Staffelkapitän of the 5./JG 52, Hauptmann Schumann, in a last briefing at Ljuban near Leningrad. Schumann, who had shot down two enemies in aerial battle, crashed into another Bf 109 before landing. When he jumped out, he struck the wing and could not open his parachute.

Oberleutnant Siegfried Simsch in his Bf 109—called "Tönchen." Simsch received the Knight's Cross on July 1, 1941 after 45 aerial victories. He fell as Commander of the I./JG 11 in France on June 8, 1944.

A briefing of pilots and ground crews. Sitting in front is Willi Nemitz, one of the oldest front-line pilots, who later received the Knight's Cross.

Changing engines at a war-zone airfield.

Feldwebel
Gillhaus tells his
comrades of the
battle in which he
shot down an
enemy plane.
Leutnant Heinz
Schmidt—wearing
a cap and
laughing in the
left background—
is overjoyed.

General overhaul of a Bf 109 motor.

For fast advances, "Good Aunt Ju" had to move the ground personnel and equipment. When things happened fast at the front, this could take place several times in one day.

Technical personnel of the 5./JG 52 before flying from Odessa to the surrounded Crimea (March 15, 1944).

Leutnant Heinz Schmidt, a successful pilot of the II. Group, received the Knight's Cross on August 23, 1942 after 51 aerial victories. By September 16, 1942 he had reached the "magic 100" and received the oak leaves for his 102 victories. Schmidt lost his life on September 5, 1943, after 173 victories in the east, while serving as Hauptmann and Staffelkapitän of the 6./JG 52 in Russia.

Congratulations after a successful mission, at the Krymskaya airfield.

The rudder of the "Red 1" shows 45 scores. It may have been the plane of Oberleutnant Steinhoff, who received the Knight's Cross on August 30, 1941 after 35 aerial victories. At that time Steinhoff was Staffelkapitän of the 4./JG 52.

Major Johannes Steinhoff, Commander of the II./JG 52, examines a 2-cm aircraft gun rebuilt for use as an anti-aircraft gun.

In May of 1942, Major Herbert Ihlefeld became Commodore of JG 52 (at left, in a leather jacket). In the right foreground is Oberleutnant Gerhard Barkhorn.

Oberleutnant Siegfried Simsch, Staffelkapitän of the 5./JG 52, was transferred to JG 1 in the west on May of 1942. He received the Knight's Cross on July 1, 1942 after 45 aerial victories.

The Bf 109 fighter planes were rolled into ruts in the soil so the ground crews could service the motors and guns more easily.

Twin-boom freight carriers—such as this Go 242—brought supplies to airfields near the front.

A Go 244 coming in to land.

The Go 244 was a further development of the Go 242. It was equipped with two 740-HP Gnome-Rhone 14 M double radial engines and attained a top speed of 288 kph at an altitude of 3000 meters. This plane was rarely used in Russia, though frequently in North Africa.

Feldwebel Willi Nemitz, an oldtimer among
fighter pilots, received the Knight's Cross on
March 11, 1943 after 54 aerial victories. This photo
shows Nemitz on the airfield in Anapa, at the
Kuban bridgehead, where he flew very successful
missions. On April 11, 1943 the brave pilot crashed
fatally at Anapa, after scoring 81 victories. He was
posthumously promoted to Leutnant.

Feldwebel Nemitz (right) sharing experiences with
comrades. The 5th Staffel of JG 52 was based at
Anapa from April 27 to August 13, 1943.

Four pilots of the II./JG 52 who wore the Knight's Cross, on duty in the southern sector of the Eastern Front in the late summer of 1942. From left to right: Feldwebel Alfred Grislawski (Knight's Cross 7/1/42 after 40 victories), Oberfeldwebel Heinrich Füllgrabe (Knight's Cross 10/2/42 after 52), Unteroffizier Karl Gratz (Knight's Cross 7/1/42 after 54), and Feldwebel Karl Steffen (Knight's Cross 7/1/42 after 44).

Since hair grows at the front lines too, the Staffel barber always had work to do. Here at Anapa, near the Kuban bridgehead, the usual rule applied: "Stand in line and wait your turn."

From September 22, 1942 to January 6, 1943 the 5th Staffel operated over the Caucasus area. Its base was at Maikop. Both pictures show the airfield with the Staffel's planes and the tents for personnel and equipment. In the background are the Caucasus Mountains.

Jakob Norz flew on the Arctic front in the famous 6th Staffel of JG 5. Concentrating on the welfare of his Staffel comrades, he climbed the ladder of success slowly.

Rudi Linz, a Thuringian by birth, was also a soft-spoken, reliable pilot on Jagdgeschwader 5. He flew in the 12th Staffel until he met his death in February of 1945.

At Krasnogwardeisk the I. Group of JG 54 flew the Fw 190, which was the ideal plane for winter combat, having an air-cooled motor.

The young Leutnant Nowotny, who wore the Knight's Cross since September 4, 1942, having scored 56 aerial victories, took command of the 1st Staffel of JG 54 on October 25, 1942, succeeding Oberleutnant Heinz Lange and, with the help of his comrades, scored one victory after another. The small white number 13 under the cockpit of his plane seems to have brought him luck.

The II. Group of JG 54 continued to fly the Bf 109—by this time the G series. The "Gustav" shown here about to take off carries two 20-mm guns under its wings as additional armament.

The Staffelkapitän of the 8./JG 54, Oberleutnant Günther Fink, served as flight instructor for the new men of JG 54. He was able to pass on his great experience as an aviator to the squadron's young pilots. On March 14, 1943 Fink was awarded the Knight's Cross after 46 aerial victories. He fell on May 15, 1943 in action against four-engine bombers over Helgoland.

The I. Group of JG 51 *Mölders* takes off from the frozen "Ivan Lake" in the winter of 1942-43, to fly escort missions for JU 52 transport convoys bringing supplies into the Demjansk Basin.

These pictures of the Krasnogwardeisk airfield show the typical Fw 190 planes, the wide taxiways and rolled airstrip very clearly.

Another JG 54 pilot whose series of successes began in 1943 was Leutnant Horst Ademeit. At his death in 1944 he had gained 166 victories over the enemy. This picture shows Lt. Ademeit at Gatschina Castle.

The workplace of a JG 52 radioman.

Changing the airscrew of a Focke-Wulf Fw 190.

 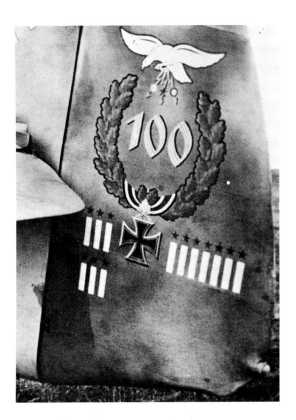

Hauptmann Heinz Bär, formerly Staffelkapitän of the 12./JG 51 *Mölders*, left his old squadron in May of 1942 to become Commander of the I. Group of JG 77. Bär scored 91 aerial victories in JG 51 and was decorated with the crossed swords after 90. The picture at right shows the rudder of Bär's plane on June 27, 1942 when he served as Commander of the I./JG 77 on the island of Kertsch.

On March 14, 1943 Oberfeldwebel Herbert Kaiser received the Knight's Cross after 53 aerial victories. He defeated 42 opponents on the eastern front in JG 77. With a total of 68 victories, Kaiser survived the war's end in Jagdverband 44 *Galland*.

Oberfeldwebel Walter Brandt, also a member of JG 77 for a long time, received the Knight's Cross on March 24, 1943 after 37 aerial victories. Of his total of 57 victories, 22 were gained on the eastern front. He defeated eleven four-engine planes while defending the Reich.

In the cockpit of the Focke-Wulf that struggles along the muddy grass runway sits Oberfeldwebel Josef Jennewein—world skiing slalom champion of 1940. The relatively short but wiry pilot with the boyish face proved himself in the heaviest fighting in the central sector of the eastern front. His series of successes began early in 1943 in a Focke-Wulf Fw 190. On February 24, 1943 alone he defeated seven enemies in aerial combat. "Pepi" Jennewein was one of the impressive "new faces" in the I./JG 51 *Mölders* in the spring of 1943.

Günther Schack—like Jennewein, a member of JG 51—also had great success in the spring and summer of 1943. He brought down his 50th opponent on July 15, 1943, and attained the "magic 100" on September 3 of that year. On October 29, 1943, after 116 aerial victories, he received the Knight's Cross. The picture shows Hauptmann Schack with the oak leaves, which he received on April 20, 1944 after 133 victories.

Oberleutnant Gerhard Barkhorn, II. Group, JG 52, received the oak leaves on January 11, 1943 after 120 aerial victories. In June of 1943 he became Commander of this group and led it until January of 1945. Barkhorn saw service only in the east and was, by war's end, the second most successful German fighter pilot.

Another pilot who gained repeated attention by his remarkable success at that time was Oberleutnant Joachim Brendel (center, in peaked cap). "Achim" Brendel was honored with the Knight's Cross on November 22, 1943 after 95 aerial victories. At the far left in the picture is Oberfeldwebel Ossi Romm, who shot down six enemy planes within seven minutes in February of 1943, scoring his 71st to 76th victories.

Oberleutnant Edwin Thiel, Staffelkapitän of the 2./JG 51, defeated his 51st opponent and was honored with the Knight's Cross on April 16, 1943. Thiel fell to Russian anti-aircraft fire on July 14, 1944 after 76 aerial victories. At this time he held the rank of Hauptmann and commanded the Staff Staffel of JG 51 *Mölders*.

Oberleutnant Thiel (right) talking with his Commodore, Oberstleutnant Nordmann.

A Bf 109 "Gustav" on a "free mission."

The Jagdgeschwader 3 *Udet*, under Oberstleutnant Wilcke, was transferred home to defend the Reich in August of 1943. "Prince" Wilcke, who received the crossed swords on December 23, 1942, had defeated 137 enemies in the east. The beloved Commodore was shot down by Mustangs near Schöppenstedt on March 23, 1944. Four of his 162 victories came against four-engine bombers.

The last mission of JG 3 on the eastern front.

Oberleutnant Nowotny reported his 82nd aerial victory on May 20, 1943 and scored his hundredth on June 5. Nowotny spent the second half of the year at the head of the most successful German fighter pilots. In this picture are, second from right, Oberleutnant Nowotny; second from left, Nowotny's Rottenflieger, Oberfeldwebel Toni Döbele.

As of April 1943, Major Graf left JG 52 and took command of the Jagdergänzungsgruppe Ost. At that point Hermann Graf was the first and only German pilot who had defeated 200 opponents in aerial battle.

Two other successful pilots of JG 52 were Leutnant Grislawski (left) and Oberfeldwebel Füllgrabe. Both gained the Knight's Cross in 1942 in the renowned 9./JG 52 under their Staffelkapitän Graf.

Although they were not fighter pilots, the close-support pilots should not be forgotten. Many of them, in addition to their notable success against ground targets, successfully fought against enemies in the air in carrying out their missions. One of the "grandfathers" of the support pilots was Oberst Alfred Druschel—honored with the crossed swords on February 19, 1943. Many of the support pilots bore the infantry assault emblem on their planes, signifying their close combat. The picture shows Druschel as a Hauptmann and holder of the Knight's Cross after 200 missions and seven aerial victories. He fell on January 1, 1945 during Operation Bodenplatte.

Oberleutnant Georg Dörffel, a support pilot decorated with the oak leaves, died on May 26, 1944 in battle with a four-engine group near Rome and was posthumously promoted to Oberstleutnant. He scored his 30th aerial victory on the eastern front on the day of his thousandth mission there.

The Thuringian Major Heinz Frank flew more than 900 missions as a support pilot and scored eight aerial victories. As Commander of the II./SG 2 Immelmann he stood out particularly in the air battles over Crimea. Major Frank died in hospital on October 7, 1944.

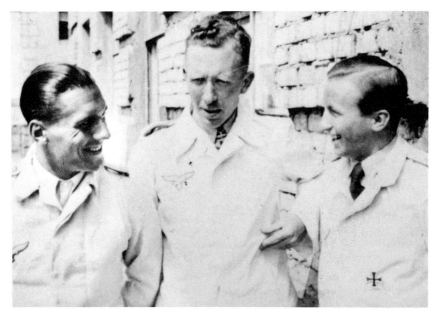

Leutnant Horst Ademeit (center) was decorated with the Knight's Cross on April 16, 1943 after 53 aerial victories. Leutnant Kretschmer (left) and Oberleutnant Hünerfeld rejoice with him.

Leutnant Horst Ademeit (fourth from right)commanded the 6th Staffel of JG 54 as of March 6, 1943, after the death of Oberleutnant Beisswenger. The pilot who achieved the Staffel's 500th aerial victory was Feldwebel Albin Wolf. Second from left is Hugo Broch, who later won the Knight's Cross.

Oberleutnant Walter Nowotny scored his 124th aerial victory on June 24, 1943. In nine days, 24 enemy planes fell victim to his guns.

In the summer months of 1943, the nights were very short for the German fighter pilots. Before it really became light, they were being briefed for takeoff.

Oberleutnant Günther Rall served as Commander of the III./JG 52 since April of 1943. In July of that year he had already shot more than 150 enemy planes from the skies. This picture shows Oblt. Rall (second from left) with pilots of his group.

Major Wolfgang Ewald came April of 1942 to serve as Commander of the III. Group of JG 3 *Udet*. He received the Knight's Cross on December 9, 1942, after 50 aerial victories. After scoring 78 victories, Ewald was shot down by Russian anti-aircraft fire on July 14, 1943 and taken prisoner.

The 2nd Staffel of JG 52 at a typical combat airfield near Byelgorod in July of 1943.

Hauptmann Johannes Wiese, Kapitän of the 2./JG 52, shot down twelve enemy planes in the Byelgorod area on July 5, 1943, raising his total score to 95. Hauptmann Wiese had received the Knight's Cross on January 5, 1943 after 51 victories.

Oberleutnant Rudolf
Trenkel of the 2./JG 52 is
greeted warmly by the
ground crew upon landing.
Trenkel survived the war
with a score of 138 aerial
victories; he had received
the Knight's Cross on
August 19, 1943, after 75
victories.

Trenkel is
congratulated by
the Commodore of
JG 52,
Oberstleutnant
Trenkel. At left is
Staffelkapitän
Hauptmann
Wiese.

Oberleutnant Heinrich Ehrler, Staffelkapitän of the famous 6./JG 5 on the Arctic front since August 1942, took command of the III./JG 5 in June of 1943. This picture of the rudder of his plane was taken at Petsamo on March 27, 1943 and shows 77 scores. The strongly camouflaged "Gustav" is armed with 20-mm guns under the wings.

Oberfeldwebel Albert Brunner, a member of the famous 6./JG 5 since April of 1942, parachuted from his plane and died on May 7, 1943. He was awarded the Knight's Cross posthumously, having scored 53 aerial victories.

Motor maintenance in the far north.

Even a marriage by proxy in JG 5.

Oberst Trautloft speaks to the pilots of the III. Group of JG 51 during the fighting at Kursk (Operation Citadel, July 5-15, 1943). At left is the Commander of the group (since June 1943), Major Fritz Losigkeit.

Changing airscrews in the III./JG 51 *Mölders* during the fighting at Kursk.

Overhauling a 2-cm gun.

A Focke-Wulf 190 of the I,.JG 54 is seen here about to take off. The three bars in front of the cross emblem cannot be explained now by any surviving JG 54 pilot.

Two Fw 190's of the I. Group of JG 54 in light formation on a "free mission" in the Wyasma-Orel area.

One pilot of the 8th Staffel of JG 51 stood out particularly in the great aerial battles in the Kursk area. He was Oberfeldwebel Hubert Strassl. In the afternoon and evening of July 5, 1943 he shot down 15 enemy planes south of Orel. On July 6 he brought down ten more enemies, plus two on July 7 and three on July 8. Then the exhausted pilot had to parachute out of his plane, but the parachute did not open on account of the low altitude. Oberfeldwebel Hubert Strassl was posthumously honored with the Knight's Cross on November 12, 1943.

On August 2, 1943 the Staffelkapitän of the 7./JG 5, Oberleutnant Theodor Weisenberger, received the oak leaves after 112 aerial victories.

A downed Lagg 5 near Orel-North.

Hauptmann Heinrich Ehrler took command of the III. Group of JG 5 in June of 1943. On August 2, 1943 he received the oak leaves after his 112th aerial victory. Ehrler led the III. Group until May of 1944 and then, with the rank of Major, became Commodore of the *Eismeer-Geschwader* JG 5.

A Bf 109 "Gustav" of JG 5 ready for takeoff.

The ground crew of the 1st Staffel of JG 51 congratulates Oberleutnant Brendel after he scored the Staffel's 400th aerial victory.

Oberleutnant Joachim Brendel dines on pea soup.

A picture of the enemy, taken during combat. The Jak-9 first saw service during the fighting around Stalingrad. The plane was easy to fly and very maneuverable in aerial battle.

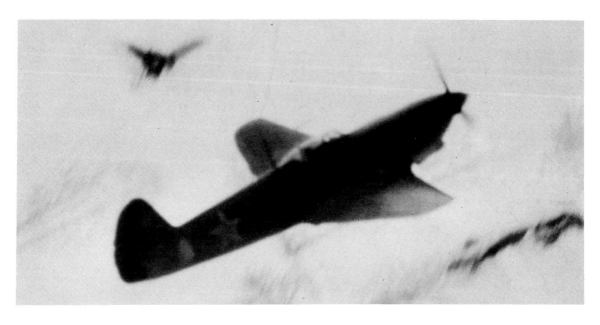

Oberleutnant Weissenberger and the rudder of his "Gustav." He scored his 100th victory on July 4, 1943 and was awarded the oak leaves on August 2, 1943 after 112 victories.

Leutnant Josef Jennewein, I./JG 51, crashed and went missing during an aerial battle east of Orel on July 26, 1943. As the photo shows, his comrades had already awarded him the Knight's Cross. He scored 86 victories and was posthumously awarded the Knight's Cross on December 5, 1943.

The fight was hard for the newly appointed Commander of the I./JG 54, Oberleutnant Walter Nowotny. On August 13 he shot down nine planes, raising his score to 137 victories, and added three more on August 14.

Hauptmann Günther Rall, who already wore the oak leaves, became the third German fighter pilot to score 200 aerial victories on August 29, 1943. His comrades of the III./JG 52, particularly his mechanics, happily took part in the celebration. Hauptmann Rall was awarded the crossed swords on September 12, 1943.

Congratulating Hauptmann Rall are Generaloberst Dessloch (left) and the Commodore of the squadron, Oberstleutnant Dieter Hrabak (right), under whom Rall served as a Group Commander.

A happy group picture with the new recipient of the crossed swords. In the center is Commodore Hrabak, to the left beside him are Leutnant Zwernemann, who received the oak leaves on October 31, 1942 after 101 victories, and Hauptmann Rall.

Hauptmann Johannes Wiese scored his 100th aerial victory on July 10, 1943. At this time Hauptmann Wiese led the 2nd Staffel, and as of October 1943 he took command of the I. Group of JG 52.

Hauptmann Max Stotz, Staffelkapitän of the 5./JG 54, has been missing since August 19, 1943. Since the war began in 1939, Stotz served in the II. Group of JG 54, ranking among the squadron's best and most reliable pilots. He received the Knight's Cross on June 19, 1942 after 53 aerial victories, and the oak leaves on October 30, 1942, after his 100th victory. Until his last mission, Hauptmann Stotz had been victorious in 189 aerial battles. The picture shows Stotz after his 500th mission.

Feldwebel Hans Döbrich was decorated with the Knight's Cross on September 19, 1943 after 52 aerial victories. Döbrich also flew in the famous 6./JG 5 on the Arctic front. After 65 victories he was shot down by Russian planes and rescued with severe wounds. Hans Döbrich was unable to return to active service.

Leutnant Erich Hartmann of the 9th Staffel of JG 52 scored his 100th aerial victory on September 20, 1943. This picture was taken at Novosaporovi on October 2, 1943, after he shot down his 121st opponent, a Lagg-5.

218 Aerial Victories

Hauptmann Nowotny at the head of all German fighter pilots

The Führer presented the oak leaves with swords to the Knight's Cross of the Iron Cross to Hauptmann Walter Nowotny, Group Commander in a fighter squadron, on September 22, 1943 after his 218th aerial victory, with which he placed himself at the head of all fighter pilots, as the 37th soldier of the German Wehrmacht (to receive the swords). Tenacity, toughness and indefatigable fighting spirit characterize the brave man whose element is battle and whose constant companion is victory.

218 Luftsiege

Hauptmann Nowotny an der Spitze aller deutschen Jagdflieger

Der Führer verlieh am 22. September 1943 dem Hauptmann Walter Nowotny, Gruppenkommandeur in einem Jagdgeschwader, nach seinem 218. Luftsieg, mit dem er sich an die Spitze aller Jagdflieger setzte, als 37. Soldaten der deutschen Wehrmacht das Eichenlaub mit Schwertern zum Ritterkreuz des Eisernen Kreuzes. Zähigkeit, Härte und unübertrefflicher Angriffsgeist zeichnen den Kühnen aus, dessen Element der Kampf und dessen ständiger Begleiter der Sieg ist

PK-Aufn. Kriegsberichter Klose, Richter (HH 3)

On September 22, 1943 Hauptmann Nowotny was decorated with the crossed swords on the occasion of his 218th aerial victory. Here are some dates that show this fighter pilot's upward path to the leading position among all German fighter pilots:

August 13, 1943: Oblt. Nowotny, Knight's Cross bearer, defeats nine Russian planes, attaining 137 victories.

August 18, 1943: Oblt. Nowotny defeats his 150th opponent.

August 21, 1943: Oblt. Nowotny defeats seven Soviet planes and attains his 161st victory—Nowotny becomes Group Commander (I./JG 54).

Sept, 1, 1943: Oblt. Nowotny defeats 10 opponents and scores his 183rd aerial victory.

Sept. 4, 1943: The oak leaves are awarded to Oblt. Nowotny after his 189th victory.

Sept. 8, 1943: Oblt. Nowotny defeats his 200th opponent.

Sept. 15, 1943: Oblt. Nowotny defeats 12 enemy planes in two days and attains his 215th victory.

Sept. 22, 1943: The crossed swords are awarded to Walter Nowotny after his 218th aerial victory.

October 1, 1943: Oblt. Nowotny is promoted to Hauptmann, effective October 1, 1943 (before his 23rd birthday).

Leutnant Emil Lang scored eighteen aerial victories in one day of successive missions on October 21, 1943. On November 22, 1943, after 119 victories, he was decorated with the Knight's Cross. After his transfer to JG 26 in the west as Commander of the II. Group, Lang crashed fatally in aerial battle against Thunderbolts. Hauptmann Lang scored 173 aerial victories in all. He received the oak leaves as an Oberleutnant after 144 victories.

Oberfeldwebel Otto Kittel gained the Knight's Cross after 123 aerial victories on the eastern front (October 29, 1943). When Kittel was shot down fatally on Courland on February 14, 1945, he had defeated at least 267 opponents in aerial battle. Thus he was the most successful fighter pilot of JG 54 in the east.

OTL Hubertus von Bonin (left), Commodore of the "Grünherz Fighters" since July 5, 1943, hears reports from Hauptmann Nowotny and his "Katschmarek", "Quax" Schnörrer, on the last aerial victories. On November 12 Schnörrer was seriously injured in a parachute jump.

Nowotny, who was awarded the jewels after his 250th aerial victory on October 19, returned to his group at the front and scored his last eastern victory—number 255—on November 15. Walter Nowotny crashed his Me 262 fatally after shooting down a bomber while defending the Reich.

With a burning motor, the pilot of this Ilyushin IL-4 made a smooth belly-landing. The crew were taken prisoners by the Germans.

Hauptmann Karl-Heinz Weber, Staffelkapitän of the 7./JG 51 since August 1943, received the Knight's Cross on November 12, 1943 after 100 aerial victories. In this picture Hauptmann Weber is talking with the Group Commander, Major Fritz Losigkeit. Weber fell in the west on June 7, 1944 as Commander of the II./JG 1. He was awarded the oak leaves posthumously for his 136 victories.

Oberleutnant Joachim Brendel scored his 100th aerial victory on November 22, 1943 and was decorated with the Knight's Cross. Brendel ended the war with a score of 189 victories. He received the oak leaves as Commander of the III./JG 51, after 156 successful aerial battles.

THE THIRD RUSSIAN WINTER, 1943-44, AND THE DEFENSIVE FIGHTING OF 1944

The Commodore of Jagdgeschwader 54 *Grünherz*, OTL Hubertus von Bonin, met a pilot's death on December 15, 1943 in an aerial battle near Vitebsk. He received the Knight's Cross as a Major and Commander of the III./JG 52 after 51 aerial victories. The beloved Commodore defeated 77 opponents in aerial battles. Hubertus von Bonin was buried in a military cemetery near Vitebsk with military honors.

As an Oberfeldwebel, Albin Wolf received the Knight's Cross on November 22, 1943 after his 177th aerial victory. Wolf, serving with the II./JG 54 since May of 1942, formerly flew with JG 1 in the West, but scored great successes only on the eastern front. On March 23, 1944 he scored his 135th victory and the 7000th of the Grünherz-Geschwader. His life ended near Pleskau on April 2, 1944 when he took a direct hit from Russian anti-aircraft fire. Albin Wolf took part in 144 aerial battles and was posthumously awarded the oak leaves. At his death Wolf was an Oberleutnant and Staffelkapitän of the 6./JG 54.

Leutnant Herbert Friebel flew with the
IV./JG 51 *Mölders* on the eastern front
since 1942. After 51 aerial victories he
received the Knight's Cross on January
24, 1943. While pursuing an enemy near
Tarnopol, Friebel crashed fatally on
May 15, 1944, having scored 58 aerial
victories.

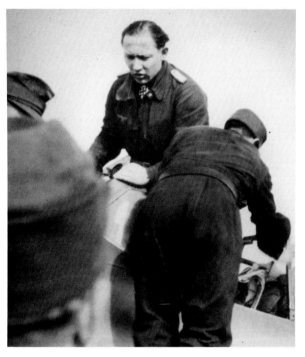

Jakob Norz—he too was an
Oberfeldwebel when he received the
Knight's Cross on March 26, 1944 after
70 aerial victories—joined the 11th
Staffel of the Eismeer-Geschwader as a
Leutnant. Here he shot down twelve
enemy planes on June 27, 1944.

Oberleutnant Anton Lindner, in the
staff Staffel of JG 51 since May 1944,
had been honored with the Knight's
Cross on April 8, 1944 after 62 victories.
Lindner survived the war as Kapitän of
the 14th Staffel of JG 51 with 73 attested
and 25 unattested aerial victories.

Airplanes in the snow. These two pictures were taken of the Eismeer-Geschwader, JG 5, in Petsamo. Both pictures document not only the cold weather on the northern front but also the attempts to give the planes necessary camouflage by painting them in original patterns.

A Bf 109, photographed from an unusual angle.

Oberfeldwebel Günther Josten—who received the Knight's Cross after 84 aerial victories—flew in the 1st Group of JG 51 in the east since September of 1942. His 100th triumph took place on July 20, 1944. At war's end he was the Commander of the IV./JG 51 *Mölders* with a score of 178 victories and 420 missions. An outstanding fighter pilot whom luck never deserted, he received the oak leaves on March 28, 1945.

Oskar "Ossi" Romm also received the Knight's Cross on February 29, 1944 after 76 aerial victories, while holding the rank of Oberfeldwebel. Romm too saw service in Russia with the I. Group since September of 1942. Of his total of 92 aerial victories, he scored 82 in the east. Along with eight four-engine planes, he also shot down two American fighters in the west while serving with JG 3. On February 18, 1945, with the rank of Oberleutnant, he became Commander of the IV./JG 3. Late in April he was seriously injured in a crash, and was in hospital when the war ended.

Anton Hafner received the Knight's Cross as a Feldwebel on August 23, 1942 after 60 aerial victories. On April 11, 1944 he was awarded the oak leaves after 132 victories. "Toni" was simultaneously promoted to Leutnant.

Next to Erich Hartmann, Hauptmann Barkhorn was the second most successful German fighter pilot in the war. Here are a few memorable dates in his career: Knight's Cross August 23, 1942 as Oberleutnant (59 victories); 100th victory on December 19, 1942; oak leaves on January 11, 1943 after 120 victories; November 30, 1943: 200th victory; February 13, 1944: 250th victory; crossed swords on March 2, 1944 after 250th victory; Barkhorn served as Commander of the II. Group of JG 52 from June 1943 to January 1945.

Leutnant Hans Waldmann received the Knight's Cross after 84 aerial victories with the 6./JG 52. Before his transfer to the 8th Staffel of JG 3 in the west during May of 1944, he had scored 121 victories in the east. On March 18, 1945 he collided with another Me 262 in the fog and crashed fatally. Leutnant Waldmann scored a total of 134 victories and was decorated with the oak leaves on March 1, 1945, shortly before his death.

Walter Krupinski led the 7th Staffel of JG 52 on the eastern front since March of 1943. In his first year of service in Russia he shot down 66 enemy planes in aerial

combat and, as a Leutnant, was decorated with the Knight's Cross on October 29, 1942 after 53 victories. On July 5, 1943 he scored eleven victories to bring his total to 90. Before he was transferred to the defense of the Reich in March of 1944, he defeated 177 opponents in the east, for which he was awarded the oak leaves on March 2, 1944. At the war's end Krupinski, then a Major, was flying in Jagdverband 44 *Galland*.

As Group Commander of the III./JG 52, Hauptmann Wilhelm Batz was awarded the oak leaves on July 20, 1944 (175 victories). Just four months before, 75 victories had won him the Knight's Cross. On February 1, 1945 he took command of the II. Group of JG 52, a position he held until the war ended; he scored 237 aerial victories in all. For this splendid achievement Batz received the crossed swords on April 21, 1945.

Helmut Lipfert came to the eastern front as a fighter pilot at the end of 1942, flew in the II. Group of JG 52 and scored 201 aerial victories in the east before he was transferred to become Commander of the I./JG 53 in February of 1945. He received the Knight's Cross on April 5, 1944 after 90 victories and the oak leaves on April 17, 1945 after 203.

On March 2, 1944, Leutnant Erich Hartmann was decorated with the oak leaves after 200 aerial victories. On July 4, 1944, after scoring 239 victories, he received the crossed swords.

Siegfried Schnell was originally a fighter pilot in the west, where he was decorated with the oak leaves on July 9, 1941 after 40 aerial victories. In May of 1943 he became Commander of the III./JG 54 in the west, and on February 11, 1944 he took command of the IV./JG 54 on the eastern front. There he died in battle with Russian fighters on February 25, 1944, after a total of 93 aerial victories.

Here again is a photo of Albin Wolf, who fell as Kapitän of the 6th Staffel of JG 54 after 144 victories, taking a direct hit of anti-aircraft fire near Pleskau. He was posthumously awarded the oak leaves on April 27, 1944.

164

Hauptmann Horst Ademeit received the oak leaves as Commander of the I./JG 54, after 120 aerial victories. Ademeit fell on August 8, 1944, after scoring 166 victories.

For 70 aerial victories in the east, Oberleutnant Robert Weiss was decorated with the Knight's Cross on March 26, 1944. In July Weiss became Commander of the III./JG 54 on the invasion front, and fell while defending the Reich on December 29, 1944, after 121 aerial victories. Hauptmann Weiss was posthumously awarded the oak leaves.

Leutnant Anton Hafner, Staffelkapitän of the 8./JG 51 *Mölders*, was on the right course to become the most successful fighter pilot in his squadron. Three pictures show his steady course to the top: After his 150th aerial victory on June 28, 1944; returning from his 600th mission (total 795), and after his 200th victory.

"Ordered to the Führer's Headquarters!" From right to
left, four officers of the day: Oberleutnant Schack,
Oberleutnant Lang, Hauptmann Grislawski, Major
Rudorffer.

Oberleutnant Günther
Schack, Staffelkapitän of
the 9./JG 51 *Mölders*,
received the oak leaves on
April 20, 1944 after 133
aerial victories. At the end
of December 1944 Schack
took over as Commander of
the I./JG 51, and was
Commander of the IV./JG
3 when the war ended. He
scored 174 aerial victories in
the east.

From left to right:
Grislawski, Lang,
Schack, Kittel,
Hafner, Hitler and
Göring.

Leutnant Heinrich Sterr, Staffelkapitän of the 6./JG 54 after the death of Albin Wolf, after his 125th aerial victory in the summer of 1944. Sterr received the Knight's Cross as an Oberfeldwebel on December 5, 1943 after 86 aerial victories. He fell on November 26, 1944 as Staffelkapitän of the 16th Staffel of JG 54 while defending the Reich, having scored 130 victories in all.

The new Staffelkapitän of the 16./JG 54 was Leutnant Paul Brandt. He too wore the Knight's Cross since September 29, 1944. Brandt stood out particularly through his successful deep penetrations and tank defeats on the eastern front. He fell on December 24, 1944 in aerial battle near Münster, Westfalen.

This picture was taken at the Skirotava airfield in Courland. The units of JG 54 tirelessly fought against the attacks of Russian bombers and fighters. At left: Oberleutnant Otto Kittel; fifth from left: Feldwebel Ulrich Wernitz (Knight's Cross November 1, 1944, after 82 aerial victories).

In July of 1944 the II. Group of Schlachtgeschwader 2 (SG 2) was operating in the southern sector of the front, which was still far advanced.

At Chersones Oberfeldwebel Buchner, pilot of the 6./SG 2 *Immelmann*, was decorated with the Knight's Cross by OTL Alfred Druschel, Inspizient of the Tag-Schlachtfliegerbände, on July 20, 1944, after 46 aerial victories. After retraining on the Me 262 jet fighter, Buchner flew aerial missions in the defense of the Reich as of December 1, 1944. He was able to shoot down twelve four-engine planes from his Me 262.

The main mission of the Schlachtflieger units was to attack and wipe out the enemy's troop and tank units. They attacked with bombs (up to 500 kg) and gunfire.

An attack on a Russian antitank position with bombs and gunfire. The picture was taken via the telescope objective.

Major Frank, Commander of the II./SG 2 *Immelmann*, examines the wreckage of an American "Lightning" shot down by his pilots.

Two experts talk of their missions: Major Barkhorn, Commander of the II./JG 52 and Major Frank, Commander of the II./SG 2.

Otto Kittel, holder of the oak leaves, visits a wounded comrade in the hospital.

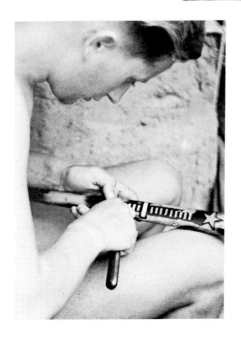

Bookkeeping on ths traditional "tally stick" by Oberleutnant Hartmann.

Leutnant Hans-Joachim Birkner—his career as a fighter pilot was unique. He flew in JG 52 and his first opponent fell on October 1, 1943. A year later, on October 14, 1944, he had scored 100 aerial victories in joint missions with Rall or Hartmann. Birkner received the Knight's Cross on July 27, 1944, after 98 victories. Leutnant Birkner scored 117 victories in all, on only 284 missions. He died as Staffelführer of the 9./JG 52 when his plane crashed on takeoff on account of engine trouble.

With all the unique accomplishments that the fighter pilots in the various squadrons achieved, we must not forget the men without whose selfless service these great successes would not have been possible. They were the men in the black, oil-smeared work clothes, who often worked day and night making the fighter planes ready for combat service. They were the weapons technicians, on whose reliable work the pilots' lives depended. They were the radiomen and intelligence men, whose constant service was often decisive as to whether the planes took off at the right moment. There were also many handy helpers such as carpenters, cabinetmakers, cooks and medics, who must not be forgotten. All of them formed a dedicated unit that made up a Staffel, a Group or a Squadron.

Hauptmann Günther Rall served as Commander of the III. Group of Jagdgeschwader 52 until March of 1944. Here he achieved his victories and was honored with the crossed swords. When he went to serve in the defense of the Reich as Commander of the II./JG 11, he added three victories in the west to the 272 he had scored in the east. Günther Rall is one of the fortunate fighter pilots who are still a model for a younger generation of aviators today.

Hauptmann Wilhelm Batz became Commander of the III. Group of JG 52 in June of 1944. Among a commander's responsibilities was that of officiating at proxy marriages, which were customary in the war years. For the "long-distance bridegroom" it was usually a case of "off on vacation." At left: Hauptmann Batz; in the center: Oberleutnant Erich Hartmann, witness; at right: the bridegroom.

Summer 1944: Oberleutnant Hartmann helps his Commodore, OTL Hrabak, put on his parachute. Left: Leutnant Friedrich Obleser, Kapitän of the 8./JG 52, and Leutnant Karl Gratz. Dieter Hrabak became the fifth and last Commodore of JG 54 *Grünherz* on October 1, 1944.

After Hauptmann Nowotny was transferred, Hauptmann Horst Ademeit took over as Commander of the I./JG 54. At this rank and in this capacity, Ademeit received the oak leaves on March 2, 1944 after 120 aerial victories. After 166 victories—almost all in the east—he had to crash-land beyond the German lines near Dünaburg on August 8, 1944, and has been missing since then.

Now and then one still finds the score of aerial successes on the rudders of fighter planes. On August 8, 1944 Feldwebel K. Dietrich of JG 51 *Mölders* defeated his 18th opponent. At that time Feldwebel Dietrich flew escort missions for the "Führer's Couriers" in East Prussia.

Leutnant Paul Brand, who received the Knight's Cross on September 29, 1944 as a pilot in JG 54.

Leutnant Rudolf Rademacher, another successful pilot in Nowotny's renowned swarm, received the Knight's Cross on September 30, 1944 after 95 victories. He scored 90 of them in the east with JG 54. As of January 1945 Rademacher belonged to the II./JG 7 and, in his Me 262, shot down at least ten four-engine planes. His total score: 126 victories.

Major Fritz Losigkeit, as of April 1945 Commodore of JG 51 *Mölders*, and Oberleutnant Anton Lindner, as of May 1944 in the staff Staffel of JG 51, listen to the first special radio announcement of the new "miracle weapon V 1."

Major Heinrich Ehrler, Commander of the III./JG 5 until May of 1944, took command of the *Eismeer-Geschwader* JG 5, replacing OTL Günter Scholz. Ehlers received the oak leaves on August 2, 1943, after his 112th aerial victory. Here Major Ehrler stands before the rudder of his plane; at right is the Staffelführer of the 12./JG 5, Leutnant Rudi Linz.

Major Ehrler awards his successor as Group Commander of the III./JG 5, Hauptmann Franz Dörr, the Knight's Cross on August 19, 1944 for approximately 95 aerial victories. Dörr, who served with

the III. Group on the Arctic since 1942, led the 7th Staffel from September 14, 1943 until May of 1944. He commanded the III. Group from May 1944 until the war's end and scored 128 aerial victories in all, including six in the west.

On August 24, 1944 Oberleutnant Erich Hartmann, holder of the crossed swords, shot down eleven enemy planes to raise his score of attested aerial victories to 301. Unteroffizier Jünger and a radioman listen tensely to the radio messages and note the exact time of the latest victory. The first enemy fell at 1:15 P.M., by 1:40 there were six. In the day's second mission,

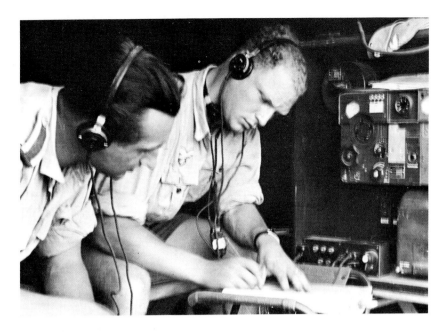

the first enemy fell at 4:00, and by 4:20 they numbered five— eleven enemy planes downed in one day.

The strain is soon forgotten after the landing, for his comrades stand beside his plane with a wreath, and there are many hands to be shaken. On August 25, 1944 Oberleutnant Erich Hartmann was awarded the jewels on the occasion of his 301st aerial victory.

Hauptmann Karl Kennel came from the destroyer planes, transferring to the support planes as of September 1942. As of July 1944 he commander the II./SG 2. This group had the task of providing support for Rudel and his armored units, a difficult mission. Kennel received the Knight's Cross on September 19, 1943 after 28 aerial victories, and the oak leaves on November 25, 1944; his total score was 34 victories.

OTL Hans-Ulrich Rudel, as Stuka pilot and Commodore of SG 2 *Immelmann*, was the first and only member of the Wehrmacht to receive, on December 29, 1944, the Golden Oak Leaves with swords and jewels. At the same time, Rudel was promoted to Oberst. Rudel's specialty, as is well known, was the destruction of enemy tanks from the air, which he accomplished with the two 3.7-cm cannons mounted under the wings. At war's end Rudel had destroyed 519 enemy tanks, scored nine attested aerial victories, and attacked ships, landing craft, motor vehicles etc.

An Me 109 with its 2-cm guns mounted under the wings retracted for the flight home. The loss in speed that these guns caused was balanced by the additional firepower. The heavily armored Il-2 in particularly could withstand heavy fire, and these guns were especially useful against the Russian "butchers."

Fahnenjunker—Oberfeldwebel Johann Pichler stands by the gun of his "Gustav." Pichler flew in the III./JG 77; on August 30, 1944 he was taken prisoner by the Russians while in hospital, at which time he had scored 75 aerial victories, 29 of them in the east. When the Knight's Cross was awarded to him on September 9, 1944, he was already a prisoner of war.

On September 16, 1944 Leutnant Jakob Norz crashed fatally at Kirkenes on account of engine trouble. The 24-year-old bearer of the Knight's Cross scored 117 aerial victories on the Arctic. "Jockel" Norz found his last resting place in the military cemetery at Parkkina. His plaque of medals is carried by Leutnant Walter Schuck, Staffelkapitän of the new 10./JG 5. Lt. Schuck received the Knight's Cross on April 8, 1944 (84 aerial victories) and the oak leaves on September 30, 1944 after 171 victories; his total score was 206, 198 in the east and eight with an Me 262 in JG 7. Major Ehrler spoke words of remembrance at the grave of his young comrade.

Oberleutnant Anton Hafner, the most
successful fighter pilot of JG 51 *Mölders*,
took off on his last aerial mission on
October 17, 1944. "Toni" Hafner's plane
was damaged by a bomb in a low-altitude
aerial battle with Jak-3 planes and crashed
fatally. As Staffelkapitän of the 8./JG 51
Hafner scored his 150th aerial victory on
June 28, 1944. Among his total of 204
victories were twenty that he achieved in a
short time in Africa, including several
four-engine planes.

This was the Jak-3. It was an excellent plane with a 20-mm cannon and two 12.7-mm
Bersein machine guns. At an altitude of 5000 meters it attained a top speed of 645 kph.
The Jak-3 was developed parallel to the Jak-9 but was put into service only in 1944.

After being awarded the jewels at the Führer's Headquarters, Oberleutnant Erich Hartmann was "forbidden combat immediately." He was transferred at once to the Me 262 Test Command at Lechfeld. Hartmann returned to his 9th Staffel—the Karaya Staffel—once, to say farewell to his comrades. On September 9, 1944 Oblt. Hartmann married his fiancee Ursula at Bad Wiessee. There followed a long vacation and then a short stay in command training at Königsberg for Hartmann, who had been promoted to Hauptmann. Here Hauptmann met Major Werner Schroer, who wore the crossed swords. His Me 262 training at Lechfeld took place only in March of 1945, but Erich Hartmann applied to return to his group on the eastern front and served as Commander of the I./JG 52 as of November 1.

THE LAST WINTER IN RUSSIA—
THE GREAT AERIAL BATTLES OVER LOST POSITIONS

On December 11, 1944 Hauptmann Günther Schack was given command of the I./JG 51. The former Commander, Major Erich Leie, took over as Commodore of JG 77. There Leie fell in aerial battle on March 7, 1945 after 118 victories (43 of them in the west). From left to right: Hauptmann Schack, Commodore of JG 51 Major Losigkeit, Major Leie, ?, Hauptmann Heinz Lange—Commander of the IV./JG 51.

Leutnant Rudi Linz, fully exhausted after his 55th aerial victory.

After 230 aerial victories, Oberleutnant Otto Kittel was awarded the crossed swords on November 25, 1944. The most successful member of JG 54, scoring at least 267 victories, Kittel was shot down in aerial battle with an Il-2 in Courland on February 14, 1945.

An Il-2 shot down in Hungary. This heavily armored craft was probably the Red Air Force's most renowned plane. Since 1942 it was used with a second crewman, using an additional 12.7-mm machine gun for defense to the rear. The "Sturmovik"—called "Butcher" by the German soldiers—ended the war with the lowest loss statistics of any Russian plane.

This Russian Major was shot down over the Riga-Skirotava airfield and was able to parachute out safely despite his wounds. At left is the Commodore of JG 54, OTL Mader, who led the squadron until the end of September 1944 and was then succeeded by Oberst Hrabak. At right is the Commander of the I./JG 54, Hauptmann Franz Eisenach.

Generaloberst Pflugbeil (second from right) with the I. Group of JG 54 in Courland. Standing in the center is Hauptmann Franz Eisenach. who commanded the group since the death of Hauptmann Ademeit. Eisenach was awarded the Knight's Cross on October 10, 1944 after 107 aerial victories. He led the group successfully until the end of the war.

On February 9, 1945 the Kapitän of the 12./JG 5, Leutnant Rudi Linz, fell after shooting down his 70th opponent. His blue "4" crashed near Horstadt, Norway. Lt. Linz received the Knight's Cross posthumously in March of 1945.

Spring 1945—Focke-Wulf Fw 190 A-8's of the 9th Staffel of JG 5 at Herdla, Norway.

In the winter months of 1944-45 a shortage of fuel became increasingly noticeable. Nevertheless, individual units flew combat missions against vastly superior enemy forces and achieved noteworthy success. Deep attacks to support the army formed another focal point of fighter service.

On March 28, 1945 the Group Commanders of the I. and III./JG 51, Hauptmann Schack and Hauptmann Brendel, celebrated the awarding of the oak leaves of the Staffelkapitän of the 3./JG 51, Oberleutnant Günther Josten, after 161 aerial victories. Josten was given command of the IV./JG 51 on April 12, 1945 and led it until the war ended. From left to right: Schack, Brendel, Josten.

In March of 1945 an experienced eastern-front fighter pilot joined the III./JG 51 in the defense of the Reich. He was Oberfeldwebel Rüffler, who had been decorated with the Knight's Cross in 1942 and now became Staffelführer of the 9./JG 51. Before the war ended, Rüffler served in JG 3 and JG 51 and defeated 98 enemies, 86 of them in the east. At right are Oberfeldwebel Helmut Rüffler and Feldwebel Slomski at Junkerstroylhof.

Leutnant Willi Hübner of the Staff Staffel of JG 51 received the Knight's Cross on April 2, 1945 after 62 aerial victories. Five days later the young Leutnant took a direct anti-aircraft hit and fell near Neukuhren, East Prussia.

The squadron staff and I. and II.
Groups of JG 54 *Grünherz*
fought bitterly against superior
enemy forces in the Courland
Basin. Leutnant Hugo Broch
received the Knight's Cross from
Generaloberst Pflugbeil on
March 12, 1945 after 79 victories.
Leutnant Hermann Schleinhege
(left), Staffelkapitän of the 8./JG
54, happily took part in this
occasion. Lt. Schleinhege
received the Knight's Cross on
February 19, 1945 after some 90
victories.

The spirit of the German
fighter pilots remained
unbroken to the last
hour. Thus, for example,
from January 1 until the
surrender on May 8, 1945
the pilots of JG 54 were
able to defeat more than
400 Russian planes in
the Courland Basin. This
picture shows them
celebrating the 100th
victory of the newly
established 6th Staffel of
JG 54 by Leutnant
Schulz.

Generaloberst Pflugbeil,
Commander of Luftflotte
1, stayed with the units
in the Courland Basin to
the bitter end. He was
finally taken prisoner
with the remaining units
by the Russians. This
picture shows
Generaloberst Pflugbeil
(center) with
Oberleutnant Gerhard
Thyben (Kapitän 7./JG
54, oak leaves April 8,
1945 after 157 victories)
and, at right, the
Commander of the
II./JG 54, Hauptmann
Erich Rudorffer (Swords
Jan. 25, 1945 after 210
victories). Rudorfer
became Commander of
the II./JG 7 in February
1945 and flew successful
missions in an Me 262.

The two most successful fighter pilots in the eastern war: Hauptmann Erich Hartmann with 352 attested aerial victories, and Major Gerhard Barkhorn with 301 victories over enemy planes in 1104 combat missions. Both flew in JG 52 and survived the hard years of the war.

REMEMBER

We do not want to forget the many nameless ones who staked and sacrificed their lives in the east during the difficult years of the war. We do not want to forget that they got into their planes daily and conquered their fear through their faith in the justice of their cause. We must not forget those who quietly did their duty and did not return home.